THE ART OF PREPARING FOOD FOR CONSUMPTION

A COOKBOOK

BY SUMER MCCAULEY

IM TOTALLY NOT GOING TO LIE TO YOU, THE SMELL OF MY DAD
SAUTÉING ONIONS FOR CHICKEN CURRY BUMMED ME OUT WHEN I
WAS A KID. I WAS MORE THAN HAPPY EATING FROZEN CHICKEN
NUGGETS AND KRAFT MAC AND CHEESE. LEARNING HOW TO COOK
REAL FOOD WAS DEFINITELY NOT AT THE TOP OF MY LIST OF THINGS
TO BE DOING. OCCASIONAL BAKING WITH MY MOM WAS THE EXTENT
OF MY PARTICIPATION IN THE KITCHEN.

GROWING UP IN A PAKISTANI AMERICAN HOUSEHOLD, THERE WAS A
BRILLIANT ARRAY OF FOODS THAT MY PARENTS PREPARED EVERY
NIGHT FOR US. SADLY, IT WASN'T UNTIL MY MID TWENTIES THAT I
FULLY APPRECIATED THE WORK THAT THEY PUT IN TO MAKE THOSE
DELICIOUS MEALS HAPPEN.

I SUPPOSE THAT OUT OF NECESSITY OF BEING A BROKE
COLLEGE KID, I HAD TO LEARN TO COOK WITH WHAT I
HAD TO SAVE MONEY. USING INEXPENSIVE AND BASIC
INGREDIENTS, I COULD COOK JUST ABOUT ANYTHING. IT
WAS THEN THAT I DISCOVERED HOW EMPOWERING AND
RELATIVELY PAINLESS IT CAN ACTUALLY BE TO MASTER A
MEAL FROM SCRATCH.

FAMILY RECIPES ARE ONLY PASSED DOWN IF YOU TAKE
UP THE INTEREST TO LEARN THEM AND PASS THEM
ALONG. IN THIS BOOK, I HOPE THAT YOU DISCOVER A
MULTICULTURAL MIX OF FLAVORS PREPARED IN AN
UNCOMPLICATED MANNER.

THANKS MOM AND DAD, FOR INSPIRING ME TO COOK
WONDERFUL FOOD.

CONTENTS

BREADS

PIE DOUGH

2 1/2 cups flour
1 1/2 tbsp sugar
1/2 tsp kosher salt
1 cup cold butter
6-7 tbsp ice cold water

- In large bowl combine flour, sugar, salt.

- Cut butter into small 1/2" cubes. Try not to handle the butter too much with your hands as your body heat can melt it.

- Using a pastry cutter or two forks, incorporate the butter into the flour mixture until it's course and small pebbles of butter are still visible.

- Slowly add ice cold water while mixing by hand until dough forms. Do not over mix, you want to see visible butter pebbles. If its a bit dry, add very small amounts of water at a time

- Separate dough into 2 balls and wrap with plastic wrap. Refrigerate for 1 hour or freeze for 20 minutes.

- When rolling dough out for your pie dish, always roll the dough out at least 1" larger than the dish so that you have enough dough to create a pinched crust.

*Let the dough sit on the counter for 15 minutes before working. Makes a sweet or savory crust.

FLOUR TORTILLAS

2- 2 1/2 cups flour
1 tsp kosher salt
4 tbsp coconut oil or lard
3/4 cup boiled water

- In large bowl combine flour and salt.

- Add melted oil or lard, mix until course.

- With a dough hook attachment or by hand, add boiled water and mix until smooth dough is formed.

- It shouldn't be sticky so add a little more flour if needed.

- Separate into 6-8 balls.

- Roll out into a thin circle with rolling pin.

- Place in a skillet on medium-high heat until bubbles and brown spots form, flipping to cook both sides.

*Makes six large tortillas or 8 small tortillas. Recipe is easily doubled.

BLUE CORN TORTILLAS

1 cup all purpose flour
1 1/2 cups blue corn meal
1 tsp kosher salt
1 1/2 cups boiled water

- Sift all dry ingredients together.

- Add boiled water.

- Mix with hands until smooth.

- Separate into 12-15 balls.

- Form by hand (or) with a tortilla press.

- Cook in hot, oiled skillet until puffed and bubbled, flipping to cook other side.

*Use wax paper or parchment when using your tortilla press for easier removal. Cook in coconut oil for more flavor.

PIZZA DOUGH

2 1/2 cups flour
2 1/4 tsp yeast
1 tsp sugar
3/4 tsp kosher salt
1 tsp garlic powder
3 tbsp olive oil
3/4 cup warm water

- Combine dry ingredients in large bowl.

- Add warm water, olive oil, mix well.

- If dough is still sticky, slowly add a small amount of flour until dough forms a manageable ball.

- Knead until smooth, about 5 minutes in a stand mixer on a medium-high setting or hand kneading for 8-10 minutes.

- Place dough into a well oiled bowl and cover. Let the bowl sit in a warm spot (or) the sun until doubled in size.

- Once risen, punch the dough down to deflate and roll into large circle.

- See grilled pizza (pg 58).

SALTY RUSTIC LOAF

2 tsp active dry yeast
1 cup warm water
2 tsp sugar
2 tsp salt
3-3 1/2 cups flour
3 tbsp olive oil
olive oil and course sea salt to top
bowl of cool water

- In large mixing bowl, combine yeast, water, sugar and salt. Stir and let sit for 10 minutes or until foamy.

- Add 2 1/2 cups of flour and combine. If you have a stand mixer: run on medium.

- Add olive oil and continue to mix. If it's still sticky add more flour a half a cup at a time until dough is manageable.

- Knead by hand for 10 minutes, knead in stand mixer on high setting for two minutes until silky.

- Place in oiled bowl and set in warm spot until doubled in size. I use cling wrap to cover the bowl but you can also use a clean towel. Preheat oven to 375˚.

- Place dough on a baking sheet oiled with olive oil and punch down into a disk shape. Cover and rise again until doubled (about 1 hour).

- Brush with olive oil and sprinkle with sea salt. Bake for 12 minutes, remove and brush water on top of dough. Return to the oven for another twelve to fifteen minutes.

- Remove and enjoy!

SAN FRANCISCO CORNBREAD

1 1/2 cup flour
1/2 cup polenta
3 tsp baking powder
1/2 tsp kosher salt
3 tbsp honey
1 large egg
1 cup cream
4 tbsp coconut oil melted

- Preheat oven to 400°.

- Combine all dry ingredients in large bowl.

- Add honey, egg, half and half, coconut oil and mix.

- Pour into greased 8x8 pan.

- Bake for 20 minutes until golden.

*Serve topped with butter or honey.
Can also be made as muffins.

CHEDDAR DROP BISCUITS

2 cups flour
1 tsp sugar
1 tbsp baking powder
2 tsp garlic powder
1/2 tsp old bay seasoning
1/2 tsp kosher salt
1 cup cream
1/2 cup butter melted
2 cups shredded cheddar

Topping:
4 tbsp butter
1 minced garlic clove
dried parsley

- Preheat oven to 425°.

- Combine dry ingredients in a large bowl.

- Add cream and melted butter, mix.

- Gently fold in cheddar.

- Drop even scoops of batter onto parchment (or) silicone baking sheet.

- Bake 10-12 minutes, until golden but not overbaked.

- While the biscuits bake, melt the butter, minced garlic, and parsley together in a small saucepan.

- Once biscuits are removed, brush melted butter topping on each biscuit and serve.

NAAN

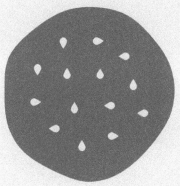

2 tsp yeast
1 tsp sugar
1/2 cup warm water
3 cups flour
1 tsp kosher salt
1/4 cup olive oil
1/4 cup plain yogurt
1 egg

- Combine yeast, sugar, water. Stir and leave until foamy.

- Add 2 cups of the flour and salt to large bowl, add foamy yeast and sugar mixture, yogurt, and egg. Stir until combined.

- Add the last cup of flour slowly and mix until smooth and elastic. Add a little more oil or flour if needed.

- Knead dough until smooth (10 minutes by hand or 2 minutes on high in a stand mixer).

- Place in oiled bowl, cover and let it sit in a warm spot until doubled in size (about an hour).

- Punch down the dough and separate into 8 evenly sized balls.

- Roll out on lightly floured surface in an elongated oval shape.

- Cook on medium <u>preheated</u> skillet and serve hot.

*Serve plain or brush with butter and add chopped cilantro and sesame seeds.

SAUCES
SALSAS
DIPS

CLASSIC MAYO

Wide mouth mason jar
immersion blender
1 large egg
1/2 tbsp lemon juice
1 tsp white wine vinegar
1 tsp dijon mustard
1/2 tsp kosher salt
1 cup avocado oil

- Combine all ingredients into mason jar.

- Place immersion blender into jar, be sure the head of the blender is placed over the egg yolk and firmly on the bottom of the jar.

- On high, run the blender until white starts to appear from the bottom, then move the blender up and down to incorporate all ingredients.

- Chill and use.

*Store the mayonnaise in a mason jar with a lid for up to 3 days in the refrigerator.

SALSA VERDE

1 white onion peeled and cut into 1/2 rounds
3 whole garlic cloves
3 cups tomatillos husked and washed
1 jalapeno de-seeded (or not if you like extra spice)
1 poblano de-seeded
1/4 cup fresh cilantro
1 tsp lime juice
kosher salt to taste

- Preheat oven to high broiler.

- Place half of the onion, garlic, tomatillos, and peppers on oiled baking sheet.

- Broil 8-10 minutes or until slight char and remove.

- Place all ingredients into blender, chill in fridge at least thirty minutes and serve with fresh tortillas or chips.

*This sauce can also be used to top eggs or as an enchilada sauce.

FRESH TOMATO SALSA

4-6 roma tomatoes diced
1 jalapeno diced
1 tbsp shallot diced
1 garlic clove minced
handful cilantro finely chopped
juice from 1 lime
2 tbsp avocado oil
1 avocado cubed
kosher salt and pepper to taste

- In a medium bowl, combine the tomatoes, jalapeno, shallot, cilantro and garlic.

- Squeeze the fresh lime juice and oil over the veggies. Give it a good mix, then gently add in the avocado until combined.

- Add salt and pepper to taste and serve!

CUCUMBER HERB SALSA

1 english cucumber
1 shallot diced
1 jalapeno
chives diced
1 tbsp cilantro chopped
1/4 cup avocado oil
juice from 1 lime
kosher salt to taste

- In a medium bowl, combine cucumber, shallot, jalapeno, chives and cilantro. Add oil and coat.

- Squeeze lime juice over salsa, salt to taste and serve.

*Great served with spicy grilled chicken or kofta kebabs.

YOGURT SAUCE

1 cup greek yogurt
2 tbsp extra-virgin olive oil
juice from 1 lemon
2 cloves garlic minced
2 tbsp dried dill
1 tbsp chopped mint
2 tbsp chopped cilantro
kosher salt to taste

- Combine all ingredients in a medium bowl and mix well.

- Enjoy as a side sauce with kebabs, vegetables, and grilled chicken.

BASIC PESTO

2 cups packed basil leaves
1/2-3/4 cup olive oil
4 cloves garlic minced
1/4 nuts
1/2 cup grated fresh parmesan
kosher salt and pepper to taste

- In a food processor, combine basil and nuts. Pulse until roughly chopped.

- Add garlic and cheese, pulse until combined with basil.

- Start by adding 1/2 cup of oil, add more oil a tbsp at a time until mixture becomes smooth.

- Add salt and pepper to taste.

- Use immediately or refrigerate for up to two weeks. I keep mine in an airtight mason jar with a lid. After a few days, a dark layer may appear on top of the pesto. This can be scraped off to find the delicious fresh pesto underneath.

*Nuts that can be used for a successful nutty pesto are pine nuts, pistachios, walnuts, and hemp heart seeds. Hemp heart seeds are very cost effective and lend an excellent nutty flavor!

AIOLI

1 cup mayo (pg 15)
1 tbsp fresh lemon juice
2 cloves garlic minced
kosher salt to taste

- Using a cup of mayonaise, blend the lemon juice, garlic and salt in a processor.

*Aioli is a great dip for grilled/ roasted vegetables like potatoes, artichokes, and brussels sprouts. Of course, its delicious with meats as well or in any way that you would use plain mayo. Aioli also can be stored in an airtight container for up to a week in the refrigerator.

GREEK BUTTERMILK RANCH

1 cup greek yogurt
2-3 tbsp buttermilk
1 1/2 tsp dijon mustard
1 tsp fresh lemon juice
2 tsp dill
1 tsp garlic powder
1 1/2 tsp onion powder
5-6 chives finely chopped
kosher salt to taste

- In a medium bowl, mix the yogurt, buttermilk, mustard, and lemon juice.

- In a small bowl, combine herbs/salt.

- Pour herb mixture into yogurt and mix well. Adjust salt to taste and enjoy!

VINAIGRETTE

1/3 cup olive oil
2 tbsp balsamic vinegar
1 tbsp dijon mustard
1 tsp raw honey
kosher salt and pepper to taste

- In a mason jar combine oil, vinegar, mustard and honey.

- Closing the jar with its lid, shake vigorously until combined.

- Add salt and fresh cracked pepper to taste.

- Store the jar in the refrigerator for up to a week, making sure to shake vigorously before using.

BUTTERNUT PASTA SAUCE

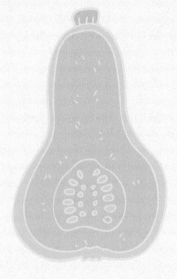

1 medium butternut
2 tbsp melted butter or olive oil (for roasting)
1 tbsp avocado oil (for sauteing)
1 tbsp chopped shallot
2 garlic cloves minced
1 cup freshly grated parmesan
1/2-1 cup water
kosher salt and pepper to taste
1/2 cup sour cream

- Preheat the oven to 375˚. Cut your butternut lengthways and remove seeds and strings. Place the squash cut side up onto a baking sheet. Brush squash with butter or olive oil, sprinkle with salt and fresh cracked pepper. Bake 30-40 minutes or until the squash is fork tender. Let the squash cool, scoop the flesh from the skin, and add to a blender or food processor.

- Cook the shallots in avocado oil until fragrant, add garlic and saute for another minute. Add to the blender with the butternut.

- In the blender, add 1/2 cup of the water, parmesan, salt and pepper. Blend until smooth. Slowly add more water until you reach the consistency that you prefer.

- Add blended mixture to a medium pot and cook at a low heat to combine with sour cream. You can add more salt and pepper if needed.

- Add cooked pasta into sauce, serve with more fresh grated parmesan.

TACO SLAW

1/2 head purple cabbage shredded
1/2 head green cabbage shredded
1/2 red onion thinly sliced and diced
1 jalapeno seeded and chopped
2 green onions finely chopped
1/3 cup avocado oil
5 tbsp white vinegar

2 tbsp honey
1/2 cup mayo (pg 15)
1/2 cup sour cream
1/4 cup lime juice
2 cloves garlic minced
1/4 cup chopped cilantro
1/2 tsp cumin
kosher salt to taste

- Mix shredded cabbage, red onion, jalapeno, and green onions in a large bowl.

- Add the vinegar and oil to the cabbage mixture and toss to combine.

- In a medium bowl, combine the rest of the ingredients and mix well.

- Coat the slaw in the dressing and serve!

HARISSA

2 roasted red bell peppers
8 dried New Mexico red chiles or
combination of dried red chilies
5 cloves garlic
2 tbsp tomato paste
3 tbsp avocado oil
juice from 1 lemon
1/2-1 tsp caraway seeds
1 tsp coriander seeds or powder
1/2-1 tsp cumin powder
1 tsp smoked paprika
salt to taste

- Preheat oven to 400° and place red bell peppers sideways on a baking sheet lightly brushed or sprayed with oil. Bake for 20 minutes, peppers should be blistered and slightly blackened.

- In a large bowl, place the dried red chiles in very hot water to rehydrate. Let them sit in the water for 20 minutes (while bell peppers roast).

- Combine all ingredients in a blender or food processor. Blend until a smooth paste forms. Add any extra oil as needed, but it should remain a stiffer paste and less of a sauce.

  *Any dried red chiles will work but the chiles that you choose should depend on your personal heat tolerance. New Mexico chiles are on the milder end of the spectrum. Chipotle chiles have a medium spice level while pequin and arbol chilies are on the spicier end.

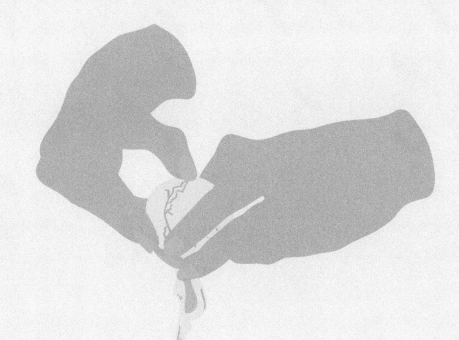

BREAKFAST

DUTCH BABY

3 eggs
1/2 cup flour
1/2 cup cream
2 tbsp sugar
1/4 tsp almond (or) vanilla extract
2 tbsp butter for skillet

- Set oven to 425˚.

- Combine eggs, flour, cream, sugar, and extract in bowl until smooth.

- Melt butter in skillet.

- Add batter to skillet and bake for 20 minutes, turn oven down to 300˚ and bake 5 more minutes.

- Remove and cool, top with powdered sugar, cinnamon, cardamom, syrup, honey, berries or other fruits.

SAVORY DUTCH BABY

4 tbsp butter
3 eggs
1/2 cup flour
1/2 cup cream
1/4 tsp salt
4 tbsp grated parmesan + more
for topping
sprinkle of fresh chives

- Preheat oven to 425˚ and melt 2 tbsp butter in a 10" cast iron skillet.

- Mix eggs, cream, flour, salt, and 2 tbsp melted butter in a medium bowl.

- Add Parmesan and finely chopped chives to the egg mixture.

- Pour batter into skillet, add more grated parmesan on top.

- Bake for 20 minutes.

- Top with arugula, spring herb greens, bacon or prosciutto.

BLUE CORN HUEVOS RANCHEROS

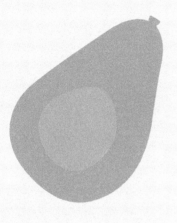

blue corn tortillas
15 oz black beans
green Salsa
1/2 cup shredded
cheddar
4-6 eggs
kosher salt and pepper
for eggs
chives for topping
1 large avocado, sliced

- See pg 8 for tortillas and pg 16 for salsa.

- Heat black beans in one pot, salsa in another.

- Place eggs in skillet with oil and fry, cook to preference.

- Lay the tortillas on a plate and top with eggs, beans, sauce, cheese and chives and avocado.

*Can add spicy chorizo or crumbled bacon on top as well.

ANYTHING QUICHE

See pie dough recipe on pg 6

One dough ball from pie dough recipe
6-7 large eggs
1/2 cup half and half
1/2 tsp kosher salt
1/2 tsp pepper

Possible additions:
1/2 cup cheddar cheese shredded
4 oz can hatch green chilies
chopped bacon
cooked cubed ham
caramelized onions
minced green onion
sautéed mushrooms
goat cheese
chopped sautéed bell peppers

- Preheat oven to 350° and butter your pie dish or cast iron skillet.

- Roll out pie dough to fit 1" beyond dish, fit into the dish.

- In a large bowl whisk the eggs. Mix in the half and half, salt, pepper, and any cheese, meat, or veggies that will be added.

- Pour egg mixture into the prepared dish with the dough and finish your pie edges. When the crust becomes golden, cover with a piece of tin foil until quiche is firm and cooked, 40-50 minutes.

POTATO CHEESE LATKES

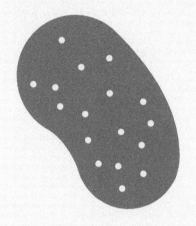

2 large russet potatoes rinsed and grated
2 cups cheddar cheese shredded
1/2 cup flour or matzo meal
2 eggs
1 tsp kosher salt
2-4 tbsp butter

- Place shredded potatoes in a clean kitchen towel. Squeeze as much moisture as you can from the potatoes. You can always transfer to a second dry and clean towel and squeeze again if needed.

- In large bowl, combine potatoes, cheese, and flour. Mix to coat the potatoes in the flour.

- Add salt and eggs, mix again until coated.

- Melt butter in a large skillet on medium heat. You don't want to burn the butter but the skillet needs to sizzle.

- Grab a handful of the potato mixture and shape into a ball. Place in the skillet and flatten with your spatula. Cooking in two batches, place up to 5 latkes into the preheated skillet.

- Cook on each side until crispy and golden, 5-10 minutes on each side. Add more butter a few tbsp at a time to the skillet as needed while cooking. Makes 8 to 10 latkes.

*Latkes can also be cooked in a neutral oil instead of butter.

ACTUALLY CRISPY POTATO WEDGES

4 medium russet potatoes
4 tbsp olive oil
1tbsp sea salt
2 tbsp old bay

- Set oven to 420° and start a medium pot of boiling water.

- Cut potatoes in half lengthways and then in half again. Then cut those halves in half again. You should have 8 even-ish wedges per potato.

- Once water has boiled, <u>remove</u> from burner and add the potatoes. Let the potatoes sit in the boiled water for 10 minutes.

- Drain potatoes and pat dry with a towel, place potatoes in a mixing bowl and coat with olive oil (about 2-3 tbsp) and old bay seasoning.

- Place on large baking sheet (drizzled with more olive oil), make sure wedges have a cut side down on the sheet.

- Bake for 30 minutes and then remove from the oven to flip them so that the other cut side is touching the sheet, continue baking for another 25-30 minutes. Remove when they look crispy and golden. Top with more salt or any other seasoning of your choice.

*Serve with a couple fried eggs and some ranch style beans. These also make an excellent dinner side.

QUICK OATMEAL BAR

For the bars:
2 eggs
1/3 cup coconut oil melted
3/4 cup brown sugar
1 tsp vanilla
1 cup quick oats
1 1/2 cups flour
1/2 tsp kosher salt
1 tbsp cinnamon
1 tsp baking soda

For the topping:
2 tbsp coconut oil not melted
1/2 cup chopped pecans or walnuts
1/2 cup brown sugar
chocolate chips optional

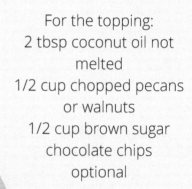

- Preheat oven to 350˚ and butter an 8x8 oven safe dish or 10" skillet.

- Combine eggs, melted coconut oil, sugar, oatmeal and vanilla.

- Add flour, mix, and the add the rest of dry ingredients. Pour batter into baking dish.

- In a small bowl, combine all topping ingredients except for chocolate chips. Spread topping over batter and bake for 20 minutes.

- Once removed, top with chocolate chips and serve with a hot cup of tea or coffee.

CHORIZO SHAKSHUKA

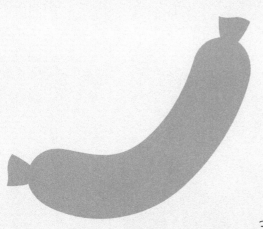

3 tbsp avocado oil
1 small yellow onion
1 lb chorizo sausage
1/3 cup harissa sauce (pg 26)
32 oz diced or crushed tomatoes
2 tbsp tomato paste
1 tsp smoked paprika
1 tsp garam masala
kosher salt to taste
4-6 eggs
feta cheese
cilantro

- In a deep skillet, heat oil and add onion. Cook onions until translucent.

- Add chorizo to the pan and cook for 10 minutes.

- Add tomatoes, harissa, tomato paste, garam masala and paprika. Simmer at medium heat for 20-30 minutes.

- On medium-high heat, gently crack the eggs on top of the tomato mixture in the pan, cover and cook 5-10 minutes until whites are cooked but yolks are runny-creamy, your preference. Serve with naan or tortillas and sprinkle with feta and chopped cilantro.

*Omit the chorizo for a meatless version. You can also use ground chorizo instead of chorizo sausage: turkey, pork, or beef all work.

SALAD

SHIRAZI

1 english cucumber finely diced
3 roma tomatoes finely diced
1 small red onion diced
2 tbsp each of fresh chopped dill, parsley, and cilantro
1/2 tsp fresh or dried mint
3 tbsp olive oil
1 tsp sumac
1/4 cup lime juice
kosher salt and pepper to taste

- In a medium serving bowl add the cucumber, tomatoes, and onion. Sprinkle in the fresh herbs and the mint, combine.

- Add the olive oil to coat the mixture, then add the lemon juice.

- Sprinkle sumac and the salt and peper to taste, mix thoroughly and serve!

COUSCOUS+
CHICKPEA

1 cup cooked moroccan couscous
15 oz chickpeas rinsed and drained
1 red onion diced
2 cloves garlic minced
1 red bell pepper diced
1/2 cup golden raisins
1 carrot grated

1/2 tsp cumin
1 tsp coriander
1/2 tsp minced fresh ginger
1/4 cup chopped cilantro
3 tbsp olive oil
2 tbsp lemon juice
kosher salt and pepper to taste
1 large tomato

- In a large serving bowl, combine the cooked couscous, chickpeas, onion, garlic, ginger, bell pepper, raisins, carrot and cilantro.

- Sprinkle in the cumin and coriander, mix.

- Drizzle the olive oil and lemon juice, mix.

- Add salt and fresh cracked pepper to taste and serve with large tomato wedges!

BLACK BEAN+CORN

15 oz black beans
15 oz corn
1 shallot minced
1 jalapeno seeded and diced
1 avocado pitted and diced
1 red pepper diced
1/4 cup cilantro chopped
1 lime juiced
2 tsp honey
kosher salt to taste
cayenne powder

- In a large bowl, combine the beans, corn, shallot, jalapeno, red pepper, and avocado.

- In a small bowl, mix the lime juice, honey, chili powder, cilantro and salt.

- Pour the dressing over the bean and corn mixture and enjoy!

BROCCOLI CAESAR

2-3 heads of broccoli
1/2 head napa cabbage
1 head radicchio
2 anchovy fillets
2 garlic cloves
1/4 cup lemon juice
1 tbsp dijon mustard

2 tbsp mayonnaise
1/2 cup olive oil
1/4 cup freshly grated parmesan
more shaved parmesan for
topping
kosher salt and pepper to taste

- Trim off the dried ends of the broccoli stalks and peel any tough outer parts off of the stem to reveal the more tender inner parts. Remove florets as close to the flowers as you can, break up the florets into smaller pieces and add to the bowl. Thinly chop the stalks crosswise from top to end and add to a large serving bowl.

- Thinly slice cabbage and radicchio crosswise and add to broccoli, combine.

- Mince anchovies and garlic cloves with the tines of a fork until you form a paste. Add the paste to a medium bowl and whisk in lemon juice, mustard, and mayonnaise. Slowly add olive oil while whisking until combined. Add salt and fresh cracked pepper to taste. Finally. Whisk in grated parmesan.

- Pour over the cabbage/broccoli mixture and toss until well coated. Top with shaved parmesan and more fresh cracked pepper, serve!

PESTO PASTA TOMATO

1 lb rotini pasta
pesto (pg 20)
1 pint cherry tomatoes halved
1 cup sliced kalamata olives
3 cups arugula
1 cup freshly shredded parmesan
fresh mozzarella balls
salt and pepper to taste

- Bring a medium pot of salted water to a boil, cook pasta until al dente. Drain, rinse, and add to a large serving bowl.

- Add tomatoes, olives, arugula and mozarella balls to the pasta bowl and combine.

- Pour pesto over the pasta mixture and coat well.

- Add salt and pepper to taste, sprinkle parmesan on top and serve!

DARK GREEN WINTER

1/2 cup pepitas toasted
1 tbsp olive oil
1 bunch of tuscan kale
handful of brussels sprouts
1/4 cup fresh shredded parmesan
1 honeycrisp apple

1 tbsp shallot minced
2 tsp red wine vinegar
1-2 garlic cloves
1 small lemon
2 tbsp dijon mustard
kosher salt and pepper to taste

- Preheat oven to 350°. Place pepitas on a baking sheet drizzled with olive oil and add salt and pepper. Bake for 5-10 minutes or until seeds are fragrant and look toasted.

- Place the minced shallot and garlic in a medium bowl, add lemon juice and vinegar. Whisk in mustard and add salt and pepper to taste.

- Pull the washed kale greens off of their stem, chop into small pieces.

- Cut the ends of the brussels sprouts and chop into small slivers, core and slice the apple into thin slices.

- Combine kale, brussels and apple. Pour over dressing and toss with clean hands to be sure that everything has been coated.

- Top with toasted pepitas and parmesan, serve!

CREAMY CABBAGE

1 head Napa cabbage
3 tbsp olive oil
kosher salt
1/2 cup buttermilk
1/4 cup greek yogurt
1/4 cup mayonnaise
juice from half a lemon
2 tbsp chives finely chopped
fresh cracked pepper
bleu cheese crumbles
bacon crumbles

- Cut cabbage into 6 wedges and set on a baking dish, drizzle with oil and sprinkle with salt. Be sure to get as much oil into the folds of the cabbage as you can. Let the cabbage sit for 1 hour prior to grilling.

- Heat the grill to a medium-high heat and place cabbage cut sides down on direct heat for about 5 minutes, then move to indirect heat for 10 more minutes or until the cabbage is tender.

- In a medium bowl add the buttermilk, yogurt, mayonnaise, lemon juice and chives, whisk together until combined. Add salt and pepper to taste.

- Place cabbages on a serving plate and drizzle with the buttermilk dressing. Top with bleu cheese and/or bacon crumbles.

SOUP

CHICKEN+DUMPLINGS

For the soup:
2 tbsp avocado oil
1 package chicken thighs
1 yellow onion diced
3 carrots sliced
4 garlic cloves minced
5 tbsp salted butter
1/4 cup flour
6 cups chicken broth
1/2 cup heavy cream
1/2 tsp thyme
2 bay leaves
2 cups freezer peas
kosher salt and pepper to taste

For the dumplings:
2 cups flour
1 tbsp baking powder
1/4 cup freshly grated parmesan
1/2 tsp kosher salt
1 1/3 cup heavy cream

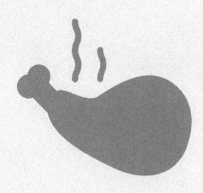

- In large pot, add oil and chicken. Cook on medium-high heat until chicken starts to brown. Remove from the pot and place in a bowl.

- Add onion and carrots, cook until the onions are translucent. Stir in garlic and cook until fragrant.

- Reduce to a medium heat and add butter, melt. Coat vegetables in flour, constantly stirring for a few minutes. Add chicken back into the pot and mix it in with the vegetables. Cook for another minute.

- Add broth, thyme, bay leaves and let it simmer for 5 minutes. Add cream and peas, salt and pepper. Continue to simmer for 30 minutes.

- While the soup simmers, add the dry ingredients for the dumplings in a large bowl. When you're 20 minutes away from eating, add the cream to your dumpling mixture and form small balls (about 1" in diameter) with your hands. Add dumplings to the soup one at a time, cook for another 20 minutes or until dumplings are cooked through. Serve and enjoy!

CALDO VERDE

3 tbsp olive oil
1 yellow onion diced
12 oz chorizo sausage sliced
4 garlic cloves
salt and pepper to taste
1/2 tsp chili flakes
4 cups chicken broth
3 cups water
2 lbs potatoes cut into 1" pieces
2 tsp white wine vinegar
1 lb collards or Italian kale stemmed and chopped
kosher salt to taste

- In a large stock pot, heat the oil until shimmering. Cook the chorizo on medium-high heat until it starts to brown, stirring occasionally. Remove from the pot and set aside.

- Add onion and cook until translucent. Turning the heat to medium, add garlic, a sprinkle of salt and the chili flakes.

- Pour in broth, water, add potatoes and bring to a boil. Reduce to a medium heat again and cook until potatoes are tender. This should be around 10 minutes.

- Place sausage back in the pot, add chopped greens and vinegar. Let this cook for 10 more minutes on low heat.

- Add fresh cracked pepper and serve!

CHANA DAL

2 tbsp avocado oil
1 sweet yellow onion
15 oz crushed tomatoes
1 tsp tomato paste
1 tsp finely grated ginger root
1/2 tsp turmeric
1 tsp of kosher salt to taste
6 cups chicken or veggie broth
2 cups chana lentils
1/4 cup fresh cilantro chopped

- In a large pot, coat the bottom of the pan with oil and place on medium high heat. Add onions and cook until translucent.

- Add crushed tomatoes, ginger, tomato paste, turmeric and salt. Simmer for 5 minutes.

- Add broth and lentils, set to a low heat. Cover and simmer for 1 - 1 1/2 hours or until lentils are soft. To cut the cooking time down, soak the lentils in a large bowl of water overnight. This should cut the cooking time in half.

- Once the lentils have cooked, add more salt if needed. Serve with chopped cilantro on top.

CREAM OF MOREL

2 tbsp avocado oil
2 lbs morel mushrooms
5 tbsp unsalted butter
1 minced shallot
4 minced garlic cloves
5 cups chicken or veggie broth
1 tsp marsala
1 tsp kosher salt
1 tsp thyme or tarragon
1 tbsp mushroom powder
1/2 cup half and half

- In a large pot add the oil, mushrooms, and butter. Cook for 5 minutes to evaporate some of the water from the mushrooms.

- Add shallot and garlic, cook until browned and fragrant.

- Add broth, marsala, salt and spices. Let simmer for 10 minutes

- With an immersion blender, blend half of the mushrooms into the broth but leave some mushrooms whole.

- Stir in half and half, cook for 30 minutes to 1 hour to let the flavors develop.

- Serve with rustic bread (pg 10) for dipping.

*Use coconut cream instead of half and half and skip the butter for a dairy free version/ vegetable broth for vegetarian/ use portobello or cremini mushrooms if morels are difficult to find.

LEMONY RED LENTIL SOUP

3 tbsp avocado oil
1 large yellow onion diced
4 garlic cloves minced
2 tbsp tomato paste
1/2 tsp cumin
1/2 tsp garam masala
1/2 tsp new mexico chili powder

5 cups veggie broth
1 cup water
2 cups red lentils
2 carrots chopped
1 jalapeno chopped
2 small lemons juiced
fresh chopped cilantro
1 1/2 tsp kosher salt
2 tsp white wine vinegar

- In a large pot, heat oil until shimmering. Add onion and garlic, cook at medium heat until fragrant (3-4 minutes).

- Coat the onion/garlic mixture in the tomato paste and sprinkle with cumin, masala, and chili powder. Let cook for another 3 minutes, constantly stirring.

- Pour in broth and water, add lentils, carrots, jalapeno. Bring to a boil and then simmer until carrots are tender.

- Turn the heat to a low simmer and squeeze two lemons over the soup. Add a handful of cilantro and the vinegar. Salt and pepper to taste and serve!

ROASTED CORN CHOWDER

2 tbsp avocado oil
1 medium yellow onion diced
1/4 cup flour
4 garlic cloves minced
6 cups veggie or chicken broth
7 ears of roasted corn / or 4 cans of corn
1lb russet potatoes cubed
1/2 tsp thyme
1/2 tsp smoked paprika
1 cup heavy cream
kosher salt and pepper to taste
chives and bacon optional

*If roasting the ears of corn: Clean the silk off of the corn and husk the cobs. Place directly on the rack in the oven. Oven should be set to 400°. Bake for 20 minutes or until golden brown. Once its done, let it cool and slice kernels off of the cob and into the pot!

- Heat oil in a large pot and add onion, cook until translucent. Coat the onions in flour and add the minced garlic. Cook for another minute, constantly stirring!

- Whisk in the broth, keeping the heat on medium-high. Add corn, potatoes, thyme, and paprika. Once you have the soup cooking at a medium boil, reduce to a low heat. Cook until potatoes are tender with a fork.

- Using an immersion blender, blend half of the soup (or all if you prefer). You can also place the soup in a blender, returning it to the pot once blended.

- On low heat add the cream, salt and pepper to taste. Serve with cooked, crumbled bacon and chives on top if desired.

CREAM OF CHICKEN+POTATO

4 tbsp avocado oil
2 large chicken breasts cut into small pieces
1 sweet yellow onion
4 cloves garlic minced
1/4 cup flour
5 cups chicken broth
6 medium potatoes cubed

2 bay leaves
1/2 tsp thyme
1/2 tsp dill
1/2 tsp old bay
1/2 cup half and half
kosher salt and pepper to taste

- In a large pot, add 2 tbsp of the avocado oil. On medium-high heat, place chicken in the pot and brown it in the oil (about 5 minutes). Remove and set aside in a clean bowl.

- Add the rest of the avocado oil to the pot and cook the onions until translucent, add garlic and cook a minute longer.

- Coat the onion and garlic mixture in flour and mix, stir for 1 minute. Add the chicken broth, using the liquid to deglaze the brown bits at the bottom of the pot.

- Place chicken back into the pot and add potatoes, bay leaves, thyme, dill, and old bay. Cook on medium heat until potatoes are soft, about 30 minutes.

- Remove half of the liquid from the pot and place in a blender. Blend and add back to the pot.If you have an immersion blender, you can do this right in the pot.

- Combine the half and half, cook another 5 minutes. Serve with shredded cheddar cheese or sour cream and chives!

CROCK OF BEEF CHILI

2 tbsp avocado oil
2 lbs ground beef
1 large yellow onion
4 cloves garlic minced
32 oz crushed tomatoes
2 poblano or hatch green chiles diced
24 oz tomato sauce
1 cup beef broth

3 tsp new mexico chile powder
1/2 tsp coriander
2 tsp cumin
2 tsp smoked paprika
1 tbsp unsweetened cocoa powder
1/2 tsp granulated sugar
15 oz kidney beans
15 oz white northern beans
kosher salt to taste

- In a large skillet, heat oil and add onion. Cook until fragrant, then add the garlic and ground beef. Cook until the beef has browned.

- Add the beef, tomatoes, and peppers to the crock pot, pour over the tomato sauce and beef broth.

- In a medium bowl, combine all spices, sugar, and cocoa. Sprinkle the mixture into the crock pot and stir until combined.

- If you are using dry beans, put them in now. If you are using canned beans, wait to put them in until 30 minutes before you are going to serve.

- Cover and cook on low for 5-7 hours. The longer the chili simmers, the more the flavors develop. Add salt to taste before serving.

*Skip the beef and use vegetable broth for a meat free version.

Main

SHREDDED CHICKEN SOFT TACOS

2 tbsp avocado oil
1 small white onion
15 oz diced tomatoes
2 jalapenos diced
1 tsp cumin
1 tsp coriander
1 tsp chili powder
salt and pepper to taste

5-6 chicken breasts
1 1/2 cups buttermilk
2 minced garlic cloves
1 tsp dijon mustard
1-2 tsp onion powder
2 tbsp kosher salt

- To prepare the brine for the chicken breasts, add the buttermilk, garlic, mustard, onion powder and salt into a large ziplock. Place chicken in the bag, making sure that it is coated with the brine. Place in the refrigerator for at least 3 hours prior to cooking and up to 24 hours.

- Grill the chicken breasts on medium-high heat until fully cooked, about five minutes on each side. Remove from the grill and cool.

- Once you have your cooked and cooled chicken, shred it and place it in a large bowl.

- In a large oiled skillet, cook onions until translucent. Add tomatoes, garlic, and jalapeno. Cook for 10-15 minutes to let flavors develop. Sprinkle in cumin, chili powder, and coriander.

- Add cooked onion/tomato mixture to shredded chicken and combine.

- Fill a blue corn (pg 8) or flour tortilla (pg 7) and top as you like using the fresh tomato salsa (pg 17) or taco slaw (pg 25).

ONE PAN CHICKEN TIKKA

For the sauce:
2 tbsp avocado oil
3 tbsp butter
1 yellow onion finely diced
chunk of ginger root peeled and grated
4 garlic cloves minced
14 oz crushed tomatoes
2 oz tomato paste
1 tsp coriander
3 tsp garam masala
1 tsp cumin
1 1/2 tsp turmeric
2 tsp chili powder
1 tsp salt
1 cup half and half
1/4 cup chopped cilantro

For the marinade:
4 chicken breasts cubed
1 cup plain yogurt
2 cloves garlic minced
1 tbsp garam masala
1 tsp turmeric
2 tsp cumin
1 tsp chili powder
1 tsp kosher salt

- In a large bowl, combine the ingredients for the chicken marinade. Let this sit in the fridge for at least 30 minutes, overnight is best.

- In a large skillet, heat the oil and add the chicken. You may have to cook the chicken in batches, too much chicken in the skillet at one time wont allow for a nice browning. Only cook until browned and then remove from pan and set aside in a clean bowl, the chicken will be added back to the sauce to cook entirely later.

- Add butter to the skillet, cook onions until brown and fragrant. Add garlic and ginger, cook 1 minute.

- Add coriander, garam masala, turmeric, and cumin. Stir to coat the onion mixture, then add the crushed tomatoes, tomato paste, and the chili powder. Simmer for 5-10 minutes.

- Stir in the cream, then add the chicken back to the pan. Cook for another 10 minutes to allow for the chicken to cook through.

- Serve with fresh cilantro on top, with basmati rice and naan.

DITALINI+PEAS

1 lb ditalini pasta
6 tbsp butter
4 garlic cloves minced
2 cup green peas
3/4 cup water
1/2 tsp kosher salt
1/2 cup grated parmesan
2 tbsp chopped fresh basil

- Bring salted water to a boil, cook pasta until al dente..

- In skillet, melt butter and add garlic.

- Add peas, water, and salt. Simmer for 5 minutes.

- Transfer pea mixture and parmesan to a blender, puree, and add back to skillet.

- Add pasta to pea sauce and add another handful of peas. Simmer for another 5 minutes and serve.

- Serve with more grated parmesan and chopped basil to top.

SHAKEY BAKEY THIGHS

Chicken coating:
2 cups panko breadcrumbs
1 cup flour
2 tsp cornstarch
2 tsp paprika
2 tsp onion powder
1 tsp garlic powder
2 tsp old bay
2 tsp sugar
1 tsp poultry seasoning
2 tsp kosher salt
10 tsp avocado oil

8 medium chicken thighs
2-3 eggs

- Preheat oven to 375˚ and grease large baking sheet or any other large oven safe dish.

- Mix dry chicken coating ingredients <u>and</u> avocado oil in a large bowl.

- In a small bowl, beat the eggs. One thigh at a time, dip into the egg and then into the breadcrumb bowl. Once completely coated, place on prepared baking sheet.

- If you have leftover panko mixture, you can put it in a container or bag and preserve it in the freezer for next time.

- Bake for 1 hour or until coating on chicken has a dry, golden appearance.

GRILLED PIZZA

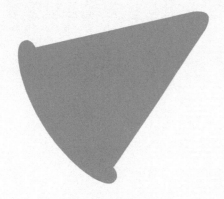

pizza dough (pg 9)
olive oil for drizzling
tomato sauce (or) fresh pesto (pg 20)
mozzarella shredded or sliced
fresh basil

Additional toppings: pepperoni, salami, prosciutto, black olives,
roasted red peppers, sliced mushrooms, thinly sliced onion,
pretty much anything

- Once you have your dough ready, roll it out to the size and shape that you like. Place onto a floured baking sheet or pizza stone to more easily transfer your dough to the grill.

- Place dough on the preheated grill (medium heat), cook until the dough has some light grill marks (a few minutes with the grill lid closed). Check it frequently to avoid burning. You don't want to overcook the dough just yet.

- Bring the lightly grilled dough back to the kitchen! Place sauce, cheese, and toppings. Return to the grill and cook on medium heat until cheese has melted and toppings are cooked. This should take about 4-8 minutes.

- Cooking time depends on how thick or thin your crust is and how many toppings you put on your crust. Being present and checking on your pizza throughout the entire cooking process is a must.

PAKISTANI STREET CORN

4-6 ears of corn
avocado oil
2 limes cut into wedges
2 tsp paprika
1 tsp chili powder
1/2 tsp garlic powder
1 tsp sea salt
black pepper

- Get that grill fired up to a medium-high heat.

- In a small bowl combine spices.

- Shuck the ears of corn and brush with avocado oil.

- Take a lime wedge dipped in the spice mix and rub onto ears of corn.

- Grill the corn until slightly charred, about 10 minutes. Serve with extra lime slices.

KOFTA KEBAB

1 yellow onion
3 garlic cloves
1/2 cup combined herbs: parsley, mint, and cilantro
1lb ground beef
1 1/2lb ground lamb

1/2 tsp chili powder
1 tsp sumac
1 1/2 tsp allspice
1/2 tsp green cardamom
1/2 tsp kosher salt

- In a food processor, add onion, garlic, and mixed herbs. Pulse until well combined and smooth.

- Place meat in a large bowl, add all dry spices and combine.

- Add the blended onion/garlic mixture to the meat mixture and combine.

- Grabbing a handful of the mixture, form long log shapes, about 4".Place on a parchment lined plate. You can cover them and refrigerate until you are ready to cook.

- To grill: Cook over well heated coals until lightly charred, about 10 minutes. Be sure to turn the kebabs to get an even crust all the way around each kebab.

- To oven bake: If you have an oven safe rack to fit on top of a baking sheet, place kebabs on the rack and bake for 20-25 minutes at 375°. Without a rack, you may have to flip halfway through cooking to get an even crust.

- Serve with shirazi (pg 37), naan (pg 13), yogurt sauce (pg 19), and tomato wedges.

SPICY WHOLE GRILLED CHICKEN

1 Whole chicken
2 limes juiced

Rub:
2 tbsp Mexican oregano
2 tbsp cumin
2 tsp chili lime seasoning optional
2 tsp kosher salt
1/2 tsp pepper
1 tsp chili powder
1 1/2 tsp garlic
1 tsp paprika

- Fire up that grill to a medium-high heat (or) preheat oven to 375°.

- In a medium bowl, mix spices together.

- Place the chicken in a large bowl and cover in lime juice.

- Rub on a generous amount of the spice mixture.

- Grill or bake, checking the internal temperature of the chicken with a meat thermometer after 1 hour. Chicken should be at 165° internal temperature.

*You can also quarter up the whole chicken and grill that way. The chicken will take on more flavor if left to marinate in the fridge for at least 1 hour. Ideally, marinate overnight.

ONE POT CHICKEN CURRY

1 large yellow onion chopped
3 tbsp avocado oil
6-8 tomatoes diced
2 poblano chili diced
2 tbsp fresh minced ginger
4 large minced garlic cloves
8-10 boneless skinless chicken thighs
Juice from one lemon
32 oz. chicken stock

el pato hot tomato sauce (optional)
3 unpeeled russet potatoes cut into 1" squares
1/4 cup chopped cilantro
1 tbsp garam masala
1/2 tsp cumin
1 tsp coriander
1/2 tsp turmeric
kosher salt to taste

2 cups cooked basmati rice for serving

- In a large stock pot, saute onion in avocado oil until brown.

- Add tomatoes and peppers, cook for 5 minutes.

- Add garlic and ginger, cook another few minutes.

- Add chicken thighs, lemon juice, chicken stock, and el pato and bring to a simmer.

- Potatoes, cilantro, and spices can be added.

- Cook at medium heat for at least an hour. The longer it cooks, the deeper the flavor. It's always better the next day.

- Serve with naan (pg 13).

PESTO PASTA+CHICKEN MEATBALLS

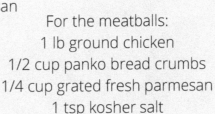

For the fresh pesto:
2 cups packed basil leaves
1/2-3/4 cup olive oil
4 cloves garlic minced
1/4 cup pine nuts
1/2 cup grated fresh parmesan
1/2 tsp salt

For the meatballs:
1 lb ground chicken
1/2 cup panko bread crumbs
1/4 cup grated fresh parmesan
1 tsp kosher salt

- Preheat oven to 375° and oil a baking sheet.

- In a medium bowl, combine ground chicken, panko, parmesan and salt. Form balls (1" diameter) with your hands and place on prepared baking sheet. Bake for 25-30 minutes.

- While the meatballs bake, place all of the ingredients for the pesto into the food processor and blend. Set aside.

- In a medium pot, bring water and 1/2 tsp salt to a boil. Add any pasta that you desire. Cook, drain, and then add the pesto. More salt can always be added to taste and extra grated parmesan can be added on top of pasta.

- Once meatballs are cooked, place on top of pesto pasta and serve!

GROUND BEEF+PEAS

1 yellow onion
3 cloves minced garlic
2 tbsp avocado oil
1 tsp fresh minced ginger
1 pound ground beef
1 1/2 cups green peas
1 tbsp garam masala
1 tsp turmeric
1/2 tsp garlic powder
1/2 tsp coriander
kosher salt and pepper to taste

1 cup basmati rice for serving

- On medium-high heat, cook onion and garlic in oil until light in color and fragrant.

- Add ginger and ground beef, cook until meat is browned.

- Add peas, spices, and cook for 10 minutes.

- Serve on a bed of basmati rice and naan.

SWEETS

SIMPLE VANILLA WHIPPED CREAM

1 cup cold whipping cream
2 tbsp sugar
2 tbsp vanilla extract

- Place cream and vanilla in a super cold bowl.

- Whisking by hand (or) using your stand mixer, add sugar while mixing at a high speed.

- Continue mixing until the cream holds a soft peak (45 seconds to 1 minute with a stand mixer).

*Freeze your bowl and whisk ahead of time if you can. The colder everything is, the better. Keep what isn't used in an airtight container for up to two days in the refrigerator.

SIMPLE CHOCOLATE FROSTING

5 tbsp softened butter
6 tbsp dutch cocoa powder
2 tbsp honey
1 tbsp vanilla extract
1 1/2 cups powdered sugar
6-7 tbsp half and half

- In a medium bowl or stand mixer, combine soft butter with cocoa powder. Mix until smooth.

- Add honey and vanilla, combine.

- Add one cup of powdered sugar and mix until smooth, then add the second cup and incorporate.

- While the mixer is running at a medium speed (or) while mixing by hand, add half and half a tbsp at a time until you reach your desired consistency.

- Mix at a medium speed until smooth and combined.

*This makes an excellent frosting for topping brownies, sandwiching cookies together, and yellow cake/cupcakes.

CHOCOLATE CHIP COOKIES

1 cup salted butter melted
1 cup granulated sugar
1 cup dark brown sugar
1 tbsp vanilla extract
2 eggs
3 cups flour
1/2 tsp baking powder
1 tsp baking soda
1 tsp kosher salt
as many chocolate chips or chunks as you wish
crushed pecans (optional)

- Preheat oven to 370˚. Cream melted butter and sugars in a large mixing bowl.

- Beat in the vanilla and eggs.

- Add baking powder and baking soda, mix until thoroughly incorporated. Add flour and combine.

- Most importantly, add the chocolate and nuts.

- Roll dough into 2 tbsp balls and place evenly on a baking sheet, **bake for only 8 minutes** and remove from the oven. Let the cookies cool on the baking sheet. Enjoy!

*Add a scoop of you favorite flavored ice cream between two cookies if you wanna be a little extra.

DONUT MUFFINS

Batter:
5 tbsp melted butter
1/2 cup cream
1 egg
1 tsp vanilla extract
1/4 tsp nutmeg
1 tsp cinnamon
1/4 tsp sea salt
1 1/2 tsp baking powder
1/2 cup dark brown sugar
1 1/2 cups flour
*Paper muffin liners

Topping:
5 tbsp melted butter
1/2 cup white sugar
2 tbsp cinnamon

- Preheat the oven to 350° and add paper liners to your muffin tray.

- Cream butter and sugar together, beat in egg and vanilla.

- In another bowl, add all dry ingredients and mix until thoroughly combined. Add dry mixture to the wet ingredient bowl, mix.

- Spoon batter into muffin cups about 3/4 of the way full, bake for 25 minutes.

- While the muffins bake, combine sugar and cinnamon in a shallow bowl. In a small saucepan, melt the butter on a low heat.

- Once the muffins are removed: One at a time, dip the top of the muffin in the butter and then roll in the cinnamon sugar bowl until the muffin top is coated. Best served with a hot cup of coffee.

CHOCOLATE ZUCCHINI LOAF

1 cup shredded zucchini
1 cup flour
3/4 cup cocoa powder
1/2 tsp baking soda
1/4 tsp baking powder
1/4 tsp kosher salt
1 cup chocolate chips
2 large eggs
1/4 cup avocado oil
1/4 cup greek yogurt
1/2 cup granulated sugar
1 tsp vanilla extract

- Preheat oven to 350˚. Coat two 8x4 loaf pans with a nonstick spray.

- Place shredded zucchini in a clean kitchen towel and wring as much moisture out as you can.

- In a large bowl, combine flour, cocoa powder, baking soda, baking powder, salt, and half of the chocolate chips.

- In a medium bowl combine the eggs, oil, yogurt, sugar and vanilla extract. Add to the large bowl of dry ingredients. Once mixed, fold in shredded zucchini.

- With a rubber spatula, pour the batter into the prepared loaf pans. Add the rest of the chocolate chips to the top of the batter in the pans.

- Bake 45-50 minutes or until a toothpick can be inserted in the center of the loaf and comes out clean. If the loaves begin to cook too quickly on the top, cover with foil for the remaining cook time.

CHOCOLATE+VANILLA SANDWICH

Cookie:
1 cup salted butter melted
1 cup granulated sugar
1 tsp kosher salt
2 eggs
2 1/4 cups flour
1 cup dutch cocoa
1/2 tsp baking soda

- Preheat oven to 375°. Cream butter, sugar and salt together until smooth and then add the eggs.

- Add 1 cup of flour at a time and mix until incorporated, then add cocoa and baking soda and mix.

- Scoop out 2 tbsp of cookie dough and roll between your hands, forming a nice circle. Place 12 evenly spaced balls on the prepared baking sheet.

- Using the bottom of a cup or a cookie stamp, press the balls down into a flat disk. Bake for 10 minutes and then transfer to a cooling rack. You'll end up with around two dozen cookies.

Filling:
1/2 cup butter softened
2 cups powdered sugar
2 tsp vanilla extract

- While the cookies are baking, make the filling! Cream the sugar with the butter, then add the vanilla and continue to cream until it's smooth and fluffy.

- Wait for the cookies to completely cool before adding the filling.

- With a teaspoon, scoop out filling and roll into a ball with your hands. Place in the middle of one cookie and with another cookie, press down until the filling has an even spread.

- Add the icing to the sides of the cookies that faced up in the oven, that way you have a clean flat looking cookie once the filling is in the middle.

CARDAMOM CAKE

For the batter:
1/2 cup melted butter
3/4 cup granulated sugar
3 eggs
1 tsp ground cardamom
1/4 tsp almond extract
2 tsp baking powder
1 1/2 cups flour
1/2 cup milk
pinch of kosher salt

For the topping:
2 tbsp butter
1/4 cup powdered sugar
1/4 cup slivered almonds
2 tsp cinnamon

- Preheat oven to 350° and coat an 8x8 baking dish with softened butter or a neutral cooking spray.

- In a large bowl, cream the butter, sugar, and eggs together. Then add cardamom powder and almond extract.

- Slowly add flour, baking powder and salt. Mix until combined, then slowly add milk. Once the batter is smooth, add to the prepared dish.

- Bake 30-35 minutes or until an inserted toothpick comes out clean. If the top of the cake starts to brown before the inside is cooked, cover with tin foil.

- Brush the butter on the top of the cake, sprinkle the toppings and serve!

BAKED GRANOLA

4 cups quick oats
3/4 cup melted coconut oil
1 tsp kosher salt
1 tbsp cinnamon
1/3 cup honey
2 tbsp maple syrup
1 tsp vanilla extract
1/2 tsp almond extract optional

Optional additions:
Coconut flakes
Chocolate chips
pecans or any other preferred nuts
dried cherries or any other fruit

- Place oats, cinnamon and salt in a large mixing bowl.

- Pour over melted coconut oil, honey, maple syrup, and vanilla/almond extract. Fold together until the oats are well coated, add more honey or maple syrup if needed.

- On a parchment lined baking sheet, place the oat mixture in an even layer.

- Bake for 20-25 minutes. About halfway through, pull the pan out and mix the oats around (oats on the outer rim of the pan will cook faster than the middle). Place back in the oven and cook until done.

- Let the granola cool completely, drizzle more honey on top if more sweetness is desired. Extra honey also helps the granola form larger clusters. Store in a large jar or any other storing container, stays fresh for a week or longer!

STRAWBERRY CREAM DREAM CAKE

For the cake:
1 1/3 flour
3/4 cup sugar
1 tsp baking powder
pinch of salt
4 tbsp room temp butter
1 tbsp vanilla extract
1 large egg
1/2 cup half and half
2 tbsp avocado (neutral) oil

For the strawberries:
3 tbsp sugar
1 1/2 cup frozen strawberries
juice from 1 lemon

whipped cream (pg 66)

- Set the oven to 350° and grease a 9" cake pan. You can grease and lay down a parchment round cut out to fit the bottom of the pan. This ensures that the cake can be easily removed.

- Sift together the flour, sugar, baking powder, and salt.

- Add the butter, vanilla, and egg. Mix. Add the half and half and avocado oil. Mix again until incorporated but don't over mix!

- Pour batter into cake pan, bake for 20-25 minutes until it's a light golden color and the middle is cooked through.

- While the cake is baking, place frozen strawberries in a medium bowl, sprinkle with sugar and squeeze the juice over them. Set them on the oven to defrost and as they do, continue to occasionally baste them with the sugary lemon juice that begins to accumulate at the bottom of the bowl. They should unthaw completely and be syrupy.

- Once the cake has completely cooled, spread a layer of whipped cream over the top and add the strawberries in syrup and serve.

CPSIA information can be obtained
at www.ICGtesting.com
Printed in the USA
LVHW071131140121
676450LV00022B/710